CODE OF CONDUCT MANUAL

Side Piece No More

Author

Pastor Robin L. Johnson

Volume 1

AN IMPRINT OF PASTOR ROBIN L. JOHNSON MINISTRY, INC.

Table Of Contents

CHAT/CHEW LOUNGE

RECLAIMING YOUR DIGNITY

CHAT/CHEW LOUNGE

RECLAIMING YOUR SELF-ASSURANCE

Acknowledgments

I thank you, YAHUAH (God) my heavenly Father the creator of all life. Throughout this journey, You've guided, empowered, corrected and strengthened me. The Side Piece No More CODE OF CONDUCT MANUAL(S), a product birthed through an ugly divorce.

❖

Family matters, In loving memory of my mother Sandra Johnson whom I love dearly, Mom may you rest in peace. Blessings to RaeShawn, Rachel, Raema, and Erik Dodson Jr. for being amazing and supportive children, I love you all dearly.

❖

Special consideration and thanks to Evangelist Lorraine Gilkes, Apostle Maria Taylor, Overseer Dr. Carolyn Mowbray, and Pastor La Rue Savoy inspirational mentors, I love you all dearly.

❖

With honored respect and thanks to Bishop TD and Lady Serita Jakes for being an inspiration to me, I love you both dearly.

To those who supported my endeavors family, fans, and friends alike, I love you all dearly.

Introduction

THE CODE OF CONDUCT MANUAL

Vision

The Side Piece No More CODE OF CONDUCT MANUAL, a spin-off from a one-day enrichment program that Pastor Robin developed to provides a safe zone for conversation, frank dialogue, with tools, resources, encouragement and motivated solutions. Charges women to reject the 2nd position in all realms of life, in a workshop setting. Topics targeting but not inclusive to sexuality, self-examination, inner healing, positive affirmations, unveil the age-long trick, why women plot to destroy other women and reinforcements to also tackle toxic self-sabotage and cancer called "self-hatred"!

Mission

The Side Piece No More CODE OF CONDUCT MANUAL enforces, expounds, and exegesis the one-day Side Piece No More enrichment program for deeper clarity and maximum self-awareness results.

Code of Conduct
MANUAL OVERVIEW

Code is defined as (1): a system used for brevity or secrecy of communication, in which arbitrarily chosen words, letters, or symbols are assigned definite meanings.

"A strategic communication that will shift your appetite!"

-Pastor Robin

Conduct is defined as (1): personal behavior; way of acting; bearing or deportment.

"May your behavior be elevated above mediocrity!"

-Pastor Robin

Manual is defined as (1): a small book, especially one giving information or instructions.

"Strive to gain information, there is wisdom in obtaining instructions!"

-Pastor Robin

Code of Conduct
MANUAL Chat/Chew lounge Highlights

RECLAIMING YOUR Dignity

RECLAIMING YOUR SELF-ASSURANCE

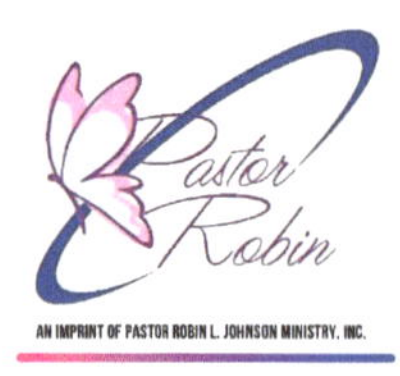

Side Piece No More
CODE OF CONDUCT MANUAL OUTLINE

Chat/Chew lounge

A clever adjoining hideaway to examine, recline, and ruminate inner thoughts, triggers, and personal behavior. Each enrichment chapter (Chat/Chew lounge) is a treasure chest of information, with at least one of these listed components:

Affirmation, Declaration, or Poem:

An **affirmation**, an affirmed emotional support through encouragement. A **declaration**, a revelation statement, a verbal proclamation pronounced with confidence. A **poem**, a writing or song stanzaic structure thoughtfully constructed to inspire, soothe and restore.

Meditation: a place to focus your attention

Each meditation, purpose/functionality challenge focus, provoke process and establish clarity. Awaken the authentic spirit, mind, and soul; true steps to structured liberation.

Focus point: a central point, as of attraction, attention, or activity.

A Focus point highlights a key observation, also lends a practical view worth notating for clarifying and/or expounding the underlined topic.

Journaling:

A Journal, space allotted to write like a diary.

Side Piece No More
Disclaimer And Limited Liability

Many may find motivation, enrichment, resources and helpful tools for personal growth; the "Side Piece No More CODE OF CONDUCT MANUAL" product is sold and purchased understanding the author nor Pastor Robin L. Johnson Dodson Ministries will give any specific financial, legal, and/or emotional/spiritual professional psychological advice. The "Side Piece No More CODE OF CONDUCT MANUAL" product does not intend to prescribe a cure or diagnose any mental or emotional illness. Be advised this manual construction does not replace seeking a professional life coach, counselor, therapist, and/or pastoral care.

- ❖ Make thoughtful consideration prior to undertaken the "Side Piece No More CODE OF CONDUCT MANUAL".

  - ✔ It's an uplifting self-evaluation process.
  - ✔ Yield to the leading of the Holy Spirit.
  - ✔ Start open-minded and engaged.

Each Chat/Chew Chapter, Chew on this/focus point, and/or meditations will challenge and inspire you. Your prayer along with the Holy Spirit guidance, a professional life coach, counselor, therapist, and/or pastoral care, the accountability epiphany of metamorphosis will yield quantum results.

Chat/Chew Lounge
RECLAIMING YOUR Dignity

Often times life events, from very highs to lows; strength to vulnerable weak places one comes through oftentimes feeling M.I.A (missing in action). Many are depleted, reach outside sources to enclasped emptiness and identity.

Meditate:
"For you created my inmost being;
you knit me together in my mother's womb.
I praise you because I am fearfully and wonderfully made;
your works are wonderful,
I know that full well My frame was not hidden from you
when I was made in the secret place,
 when I was woven together in the depths of the earth." Psalms 139:13-15 NIV

Who am I, the Woman?

The journey in discovering you may be long but well worth it!

Listed below are the honorary identity "Who am I, the Woman" code of conduct self-reflections!

1. Peel away become bare-skinned.

   ➢ What makes you smile, within your skin?
   ➢ Do you have a favorite pastime, by yourself?
   ➢ Could you describe three (3) positive components about yourself?

2. Challenge the cognizance belief of your purpose.
   ➢ Are you aware, prior to marriage, divorce, children, miscarriage, or abortion; purpose was seeded within? Those are external, the purpose is eternal.

"Adopting to the second position derives from not fully understanding "I"!"
-Pastor Robin

Chat/Chew **Lounge**
RECLAIMING YOUR Dignity

Women are described as emotional, catty, and dramatic; clearly, some women wear those characteristics like a badge. Emotions are God's creative way for individuals to feel; feel passion, horny, empathy, pain, happiness, and so forth.

Meditate:
"He that hath no rule over his own spirit is like a city that is broken down, and without walls."
Proverbs 25:28 KJV

Identifying & Mastering Emotions!

The most important key is becoming proficient emotionally.

Listed below are the honorary "Identifying & Mastering Emotions" code of conduct self-reflections!

3. Research says women emotional factors:

   ➢ During the last (luteal) phase of the menstrual cycle, which starts after ovulation.
   ➢ Women's brain chemistry and hormone fluctuations differ from men, which may make them more prone to anxiety disorders.

4. Imperative to educate yourself and identify:
   ➢ Your mental capacity, health, and strength.
   ➢ Unresolved fatherlessness, trama, and fear.
   ➢ Your triggers and vulnerabilities.

5. Master:
   ➢ Compulsions- an irresistible urge, especially against one's conscious wishes.
   ➢ Every Action- has a reaction.
   ➢ Decisions- must be skillful wisdom.

"If you don't master your emotions, they will master you!"
-Pastor Robin

Chat/Chew **Lounge**
RECLAIMING YOUR Dignity

There is an old saying, sugar and salt are both white substances however they taste, smell and function differently. How eerie are the similarities also total opposites are love, lust, and low esteem. All tangible feelings often are driven from inner reflection and exterior affection or the lack thereof.

Poem:
"I'm the queen of gems, a pearl who is authentic and pure. I no longer feel unworthy for genuine non-perverted love; I'm the queen of gems, a pearl".

-Pearls-The Core Uniqueness of a Woman ©

Your Love, Lust and Low Esteem!

Be proficiently educated, know the difference between the wide spectrum of emotional truths.

Listed below are the honorary "Your Love, Lust and Low Esteem" code of conduct self-reflections!

6. Truth is grounded by:

   ➤ Facts not feelings.
   ➤ God's Word, not gossip nor opinions.

7. Lust is driven:
   ➤ By feelings not facts.
   ➤ Immediate gratification with no regard for consequences.

8. Low Esteem drives from:
   ➤ False perspective of self-value.
   ➤ Trauma-a deeply distressing or disturbing experience.

Chat/Chew **Lounge**
RECLAIMING YOUR DIGNITY

CHEW ON THIS

Side Piece No More "Dignity" code of conduct recap viewpoints:

Dignity that governs:
- → Conduct
- → Speech or Conversation
- → Decorum
- → Etiquette
- → Self-care
- → Self-respect

DECLARATION

I am not my past failures, I am not my past loses, I am not my past traumas, I am not my past lack, I am not my past misunderstandings, I am not my past challenges, I am not my past hurts, I am not my past choices, I am not living in my past! I reclaim my purpose, self-value, and dignity today! Amen!

JOURNAL

____
____
____
____
____
____
____
____
____
____

Chat/Chew **Lounge**
RECLAIMING YOUR SELF-ASSURANCE

The Anatomy of the brain, the central nervous system enclosed in the cranium of humans serving to control and coordinate the mental and physical actions. Our mental persuasion either healthy or not navigates the Conscious and Subconscious, the mind beneath or beyond consciousness. Utmost urgency we desire a stable and steadfast posture.

Meditate:
"Create in me a pure heart, O God,

and renew a steadfast spirit within me." Psalms 51:10 NIV

Conscious and Subconscious Self-Sabotage

Illuminate your mental persuasion, most often times it's not your haters but self-sabotage preventing growth.

Listed below are the honorary "Conscious and Subconscious Self-Sabotage" code of conduct self-reflections points!

9. Crippling Fear and Doubt which causes you to:
   - ➢ Abort your dreams.
   - ➢ Smother or neglect your passion(s).

10. Insecurities:
    - ➢ Desire External Approval.
    - ➢ Unhealthy schools of self-thought(s).

11. Manipulation:
    - ➢ Looking for validation, your prey to manipulators.
    - ➢ You talk yourself out of making boss moves.

Chat/Chew **Lounge**
RECLAIMING YOUR SELF-ASSURANCE

The human imagination virtuosity enthralled with multi-diverse ideas and aspirations, we dare not douse that creativity. However, without cultivation and boundaries, it can dangerously evolve into fantasy; which real intimacy is smothered.

Meditate:
"Love is patient, love is kind. It does not envy, it does not boast, it is not proud. It does not dishonor others, it is not self-seeking, it is not easily angered, it keeps no record of wrongs. Love does not delight in evil but rejoices with the truth. It always protects, always trusts, always hopes, always perseveres. Love never fails.." I Cor 13:4-8 NIV

Sexual Fantasy vs Sexual Intimacy!

With unresolved little girl scattered barbie doll expectations; a fairy tale Cinderella waiting to be whisked off your feet. Deciphering between reality, fantasy, and authentic love can be life-changing.

Listed below are the honorary "Sexual Fantasy vs Sexual Intimacy" code of conduct self-reflections points!

12. Love is multifaceted, properly evaluate:

  ➢ Agape Love:

  Charity unconditional "God" love, unselfish pure love without sexual intention.

  ➢ Phileo Love:

  Between family, friends, enjoyment and strong friendship bonds.

Chat/Chew **Lounge**
Sexual Fantasy vs Sexual Intimacy
Continuance

    ➤ Eros Love:

    Romantic love, physical love, and sexual desire.

    ➤ Storge Love:

    Natural or instinctual affection, such as the love of a parent towards offspring and empathy bond.

    ➤ Ludus Love:

    View love as a game taking pride in having multiple conquests, won't commit. They're all about the game and excitement that comes along with a new partner.

13. Authentic Loving Intimacy:
    - ➤ Acknowledges your existence (not only via social media, an admirer, or sexual excursions)
    - ➤ Genuine
    - ➤ Invested
    - ➤ Respectful
    - ➤ Mutual loving feelings
    - ➤ Doesn't provoke insecurities
    - ➤ Doesn't inflict pain (emotionally, physically, mentally or financially)

14. Fantasy
    - ➤ Erotic (to arouse sexual desire or excitement)
        1. Be leery if often asked to mask as someone else and being yourself feels inadequate.
    - ➤ Imaginary (creates something from an imagination that is not based on reality)
        1. The imagination realm should inspire not to replace reality.

Chat/Chew **Lounge**
RECLAIMING YOUR SELF-ASSURANCE

Truly a worldwide truth, all desire love, affection, and romance. However, after the tingling zap rush of the forbidden, many feel after the scandalous charged atmosphere we discover backlash.

Meditate:
"Now the serpent was more crafty than any of the wild animals the Lord God had made. He said to the woman, "Did God really say, 'You must not eat from any tree in the garden'?" The woman said to the serpent, "We may eat fruit from the trees in the garden, but God did say, 'You must not eat fruit from the tree that is in the middle of the garden, and you must not touch it, or you will die." Gen 3:1-3 NIV

A Married Man, comes Curses, Deceit, and Lies!

With unresolved little girl scattered barbie doll expectations; loneliness, and looking for authentic love; things we've covered within this manual can be factors in considering a married individual.

Listed below are the honorary "A Married Man, comes Curses, Deceit, and Lies" code of conduct self-reflections points!

15.

In spite of the casual modern thoughts of marriage, like marriage is just a paper; not popular but true inappropriate relationships with covenant keepers (married people) can invoke costly infraction(s). These infractions are often viewed as karma, bewitched or **curses**.

Chat/Chew **Lounge**
A Married Man, comes Curses, Deceit, and Lies!

Continuance

> ➤ Curses- punishment on someone or something; affliction.

Focus Point:

"He who finds a <u>wife</u> finds what is good

and receives <u>favor</u> from the Lord." Pro 18:22 NIV

1. God decrees a wife equals favor, however, a sidechic equals/receives the opposite of favor; Curses.

Confessional Journaling: Begin to release your heart in writing!

JOURNAL

____
____
____
____
____
____
____
____
____
____
____
____
____
____
____
____
____

Chat/Chew **Lounge**
A Married Man, comes Curses, Deceit, and Lies!

Continuance

Focus Point:
"Haven't you read," he replied, "that at the beginning the Creator 'made them male and female,'[a] 5 and said, 'For this reason a man will leave his father and mother and be united to his wife, and the two will become one flesh'[b]? 6 So they are no longer two, but one flesh. Therefore what God has joined together, let no one separate." Matt 19:4-6 NIV

2. Ignoring God, subscribing that man sanctioned marriage, which the bible disqualifies could lead to a costly infraction.
3. God distinct conviction, "Therefore what God has joined together, let no one separate." Causing a breach/separation could lead to a costly infraction.
4. The "two will become one flesh", many wounds occur when slashing violently, tearing apart what God infused into "one flesh"!

*In event of harsh abuse within a marriage seek professional assistance on how to remove yourself safely, dissolve union lawfully and honorably.

Confessional Journaling: Begin to release your heart in writing!

JOURNAL

____
____
____
____
____
____
____
____
____
____
____

Chat/Chew*Lounge*
A Married Man, comes Curses, Deceit, and Lies!

Continuance

> ➢ Deceit- the action or practice of deceiving by concealing or misrepresenting the truth.

Focus Point:

"Therefore, rid yourselves of all malice and all deceit, hypocrisy, envy, and slander of every kind."

1 Peter 2:1 NIV

5. Deceitfulness a flawed character trait disposition:
   - To deceive or lead into error.
   - A practice that misleads another.
   - Causes another to believe what is false
   - A contrivance to entrap.
   - Witty deception and fraud.

Confessional Journaling: Begin to release your heart in writing!

JOURNAL

____
____
____
____
____
____
____
____
____
____
____

Chat/Chew*Lounge*
A Married Man, comes Curses, Deceit, and Lies!

Continuance

> ➢ Liar- a person who lies by saying something they know is not true.

Focus Point:
"The Lord detests lying lips,

  but he delights in people who are trustworthy."

Pro 12:22 NIV

6. Lying is a flawed character trait disposition:
   - Manipulative, Manipulators frequently tell lies, tend to persist in lying even when challenged to tell the truth, and don't feel uncomfortable or guilty when lying.
   - Natural and guiltless performers.
   - Demonstrate emotional camouflage.
   - Physically attractive, confident and experienced.

Confessional Journaling: Begin to release your heart in writing!

JOURNAL

____
____
____
____
____
____
____
____
____
____
____

Chat/Chew **Lounge**
RECLAIMING YOUR SELF-ASSURANCE

Humanity is diverse culturally, socially, economically and so forth. Which makes the landscape of relationships and love dynamic.

Meditate:
"Be completely humble and gentle; be patient, bearing with one another in love."

Eph 4:2 NIV

Reclaim & Restore Relationships!

Created to be purposeful, inspiring and loving, God designed humanity to be relational; we discover life is empty without genuine relationships!

Listed below are the honorary "Reclaim & Restore Relationships" code of conduct self-reflections points

16.

Reclaim Restorative Relationships character trait disposition:

➢ Have a genuine attraction and connection.
➢ Have good communication and defined understanding.
➢ Are attentive and understanding.
➢ Loyalty and shows reciprocal acts of kindness.

Confessional Journaling: Begin to release your heart in writing!

JOURNAL

____
____
____
____
____
____
____

Chat/Chew *Lounge*
RECLAIMING YOUR SELF-ASSURANCE

CHEW ON THIS

Side Piece No More "Self-Assurance" code of conduct recap viewpoints:

Self-Assurance that governs:
→ Inner Confidence
→ Rejects Desperation
→ Demands Authentic Love
→ Provokes Excellence

DECLARATION

I am adored, I am beautiful, I am courageous, I am confident, I am consistent, I am creative, I am enduring, I am inestimable, I am impeccable! I reclaim my confidence, purpose, and self-assurance today! Amen!

JOURNAL

____
____
____
____
____
____
____
____
____
____

That concludes the "Side Piece No More CODE OF CONDUCT MANUAL" Vol.1

We pray it was life-changing for you.

About The Author

Robin reared in a single-parent household by Sandra Johnson, in a close net community in the suburbs of Maryland. Robin discovered her calling and interest in helping the disadvantaged and disenfranchised at a young age. A passion birthed after knowing her mother Sandra was displaced from her siblings after the death of her sick mother, placed into the foster care system but blessed to be raised by Mr. and Mrs. George Herman Jackson, a loving couple whom Robin recognizes as her loving, devoted grandparents. Robin's mother ironically became a foster parent, where Robin found herself helping to raise countless foster children.

Robin has been an asset to countless children, youth, and women ministries alike; served in the capacity of a Praise and Worship Leader, Youth empowerment Leader, Teacher, Prophetess, Minister, and Elder. A great milestone, Aug 31, 2012, Robin would be installed to serve Created with Promise and Potential Ministries as Pastor located in Hampton GA. later renamed Created To Win International; the main hub housed in Charlotte, NC.

Robin, a mother of four; cherishes family her first passion. The second passion unmistakably is serving people, singing gospel music, and delivering the gospel. Robin co-founded Refuge Ministries in 1995, participated in established non- profit organization boards, each main focus target the issues of the lost and forsaken. Robin understands the power of prayer and intercession, she co-founded Building Kingdom Walls Intercessors in June 2012 and founded Fresh Fire Breakthrough Prayer January 2013.

Clearly, everyone that is acquainted with her knows, women's enrichment and sisterhood are at the top of her list as well, there is the birthing of Woman to Woman Impartation (WTWI) annual conference and ministry in 2012 and Side Piece No More (SPNM) in 2017. Robin has a multifaceted diverse background; administration, management, finance, facilitator, organizational development skills, event planning, and an entrepreneur.

Robin believes her eyes have not seen nor her ears have heard; what YAH (God) has yet to reveal concerning her life.

References

Side Piece No More CODE OF CONDUCT MANUAL Volume 1

Among a calibration of Side Piece No More CODE OF CONDUCT MANUAL series.

Copyright © 2020 by Pastor Robin L. Dodson Johnson

Scriptures are taken from the New International Version (NIV)

Holy Bible, New International Version®, NIV®

Copyright ©1973, 1978, 1984, 2011 by Biblica, Inc.® All rights reserved worldwide.